Drowning, Resurfacing

notes on heartbreak & healing

Frankie Riley

This is for the ones who are broken hearted.
For the ones with the soft souls, who were made to
feel as though they are too sensitive, too *feeling*.
For the ones who loved the wrong person, but still
hold onto the hope of finding the right one.
For the ones who were made to feel like they are too
difficult to love, just for asking for the bare minimum.
For the ones whose hearts were shattered by
someone they thought was their soulmate.
For the ones who are fighting for their healing.
For the ones who need a reminder of what they truly
deserve.

This is for *you*.

TABLE of CONTENTS

PART ONE – *drowning*:

PART TWO – *resurfacing*:

PART ONE:

Drowning

Drowning [*n.*]: being submerged and unable to
breathe; the physical feeling of being engulfed or
overwhelmed by something.

The Waves of Heartbreak

From what I know of heartbreak, it comes in a series of waves. Some gentle and calm, softly brushing over you to wash away the lingering hurt. And some harsh and rough, brutally dragging you to the darkest depths of grief and despair.

First comes an overwhelming wave of *numbness*. In the immediate aftermath of the breakup, you don't really feel anything, nothing other than detachment. You're slowly drowning, being pulled deeper and deeper into some dark corner of your soul; but you don't fight it. You allow the darkness to consume you, a way to remove yourself from reality, to shield your heart from acknowledging and accepting the breakup – *and* the emotions that come with it. You're just living in survival mode, going through the motions each day completely void of feeling, becoming a shell of the person you once were.

Then sooner or later, little cracks begin to appear in that numbness, until all those emotions you've been avoiding come rushing to the surface. Mainly, an overwhelming sense of *sadness*. The pain of the breakup hits you like a tidal wave, with enough force to knock the wind out of you. With each inhale it gets harder to breathe, as though you're drowning in grief. Endless nights are spent crying yourself to sleep, desperately wishing things didn't have to be this way. You can't yet begin to comprehend that this pain is the start of a new beginning, because right now it just feels like an all-consuming end.

Then comes the waves of rumination and anger, to forcefully crash against your sanity. You replay every moment of the relationship in your mind, the beautiful and the ugly, trying to figure out when and *how* it went so very wrong. You're constantly plagued with the *what ifs*, creating a tsunami of anger within you – anger at them, and anger at yourself. You mentally torture yourself with the *'I should have… why did he… but we could have…'* over and over, until you feel like screaming in frustration.

For a while, the only way to cope with all of those overwhelming feelings is to live in a sense of *denial*, especially if the breakup was unexpected and the rug was suddenly pulled out from under you. Even if you know, deep down in your heart, that they were not *your person*; you cling onto the hope that there will be a future with them. That your souls will eventually find their way back to one another – someday, somehow, somewhere. You hold onto that hope with every fibre of your being, because it's the only thing that helps you make it through the darkest days of the breakup.

But eventually there comes a point where you must accept that it's over. That this truly *is* the end, and this is how things were always supposed to work out. Acknowledging and accepting this truth is one of the hardest things you will ever have to do, sometimes hurting you more than the initial breakup – because that hope you've been frantically holding onto has been severed. Even if you were the one who decided to end the relationship, it still hurts sometimes to accept that they will never again be a part of your life.

But I want you to know that no storm can last forever. With time, you start to resurface from the grief with a sense of hope in your heart, and an *acceptance* of the old reality that must now be left in the past. Where there were once enormous waves of sadness and anger dragging you to the depths of despair, now there are only gentle waves of peace and clarity. Little by little, day by day, they slowly dance against you, healing you with each touch, washing away the leftover remnants of heartache.

Some days you still feel a drop of that pain, somewhere deep inside your heart. But you are slowly learning to appreciate the pain, because it reminds you that the love you felt was *real.* That you deeply loved someone and were loved in return – even if it was just for a while.

Reasons We Hold On (When We Know We Need to Let Go)

Sometimes, we hold on to those we are not meant to love – for all the wrong reasons.

Sometimes, we hold on because we have already invested so much into the relationship. We gave our precious time, our effort and energy, our entire hearts. So, if we let them go, we believe that it will all have been for nothing. That everything we poured into the relationship will be a complete waste.

Sometimes, we hold on because we convince ourselves that things will change for the better. That maybe *they* will change – if only we have enough patience, if only we continue to love them fiercely enough.

Sometimes, we hold on because we are truly afraid of being alone again, even more so when the relationship is long-term. We forget that being alone does in no way equate to *loneliness*. Or maybe we have been attached to them for so long that our lives have blended into one, forcing us to lose our own identity – so much so that we don't remember how to function without them.

Sometimes, we hold on because the love has consumed every part of our heart and soul, clouding all logic and reason. Despite our needs not being met, we can't imagine ever being capable of loving someone else again, or as much as we love them.

Sometimes, we hold on because we don't believe we are worthy of more – of a healthy love. Over time, the relationship has chipped away at our self-worth and self-esteem. So much so, that we accept love in half measures because we think it is all we deserve.

Sometimes, we hold on because the relationship has become our comfort zone, our familiar routine, our stability. And so, the thought of starting over is incredibly daunting. We choose to stay in the unhappiness of the known, because we are so afraid of jumping into the *unknown*.

But please understand that holding on to those you are not meant to love will hurt so much more than letting them go. I know you're afraid to walk away, but sometimes losing someone is the only way to find *yourself*.

Loving A Narcissist Feels Like This

Loving a narcissist is to relentlessly ask yourself the question *do they really love me?* I know it hurts to hear this, but they are capable of loving you – just not in the same way that you love them. Not in a heathy way. And not in the way that you deserve. Narcissists see love as a transaction, so their love for you will only ever be *conditional*, depending solely on what they can get from you. The decision to show you love is always for their own benefit, generally for the desire and attention they receive in return. The fuel they need to satisfy their ego.

Loving a narcissist is to never have your emotional needs met, because they don't have the emotional capacity to meet those needs. Narcissists often have a complete lack of *empathy* for other's feelings – the foundation of their personalities. Therefore, it's incredibly easy for them to act sweet and loving one moment, then as cold as ice the next. They lack the basic empathy needed to care about, or even recognise, how their words and actions impact you. The reality is, they are the centre of their own universe. So, they expect everyone around them to accommodate their

14

feelings, without ever considering the feelings of others.

Loving a narcissist is to always feel like you're not good enough. It does not matter how much love and energy you pour into the relationship; they will still find ways to tear you down – because they *thrive* on making you feel like the lesser person. They play on your insecurities, slowly chipping away at your self-esteem until you feel paralysing self-doubt. Please understand that these criticisms have nothing to do with you and your worth, they are a reflection of their own deep insecurities. They vilify you to make themselves feel better, a way to satisfy their deep-rooted need to be superior.

Loving a narcissist is to live on a highly emotional rollercoaster. At first, the relationship is intensely passionate, they shower you with attention in order to gain your deepest admiration in return. But once the initial burning passion starts to fade, and you settle into a calm and contented relationship, they become deeply uncomfortable. They thrive off intensity, so when that begins to disappear, they will find ways to create tension and pick fights with you. *Chaos* is their comfort. The reality is, they cannot handle the authenticity of a serious relationship, because they would need to open themselves up and be vulnerable – something they don't have the emotional capacity to do. And so, it's easier for them to destroy the relationship by attacking you and blaming you for their insecurities.

Loving a narcissist is to persistently question your reality, and the validity of your feelings. No matter how much hurt they cause you, *you* will always be the problem in their eyes. Narcissists tend to see themselves as the victim, and because of that, they need a villain in their story. Their lack of emotional responsibility means that every problem, every fight, every stressor, and every insecurity will always be blamed on you. And when your feelings and reality are continuously gaslighted in this way, then *you too* start to believe that you are the problem. That you are taking the things they say out of context, because you are 'too emotional.' That the way they treat you is 'not that bad'. That the constant fights and chaos are your fault for being such a terrible partner, and failing to meet their needs.

Loving a narcissist is to step into a fire and watch every inch of yourself burn to ruins – mentally, emotionally, and spiritually.

The Confusion of Betrayal

I am sorry that you gave your heart to someone who betrayed your trust, just for a moment of pleasure with someone else. I know how devastating it feels to discover that the one you are in love with has deceived you in the worst way – like a punch to your stomach, knocking the wind out of you with such force. Your entire reality shattering in an instant, along with all the promises they made to you.

You never deserved to go through this, and I hope you know that it was *not* your fault. Infidelity occurs even in happy and healthy relationships, so please don't blame yourself, or torture your mind thinking there was something you could have done differently to prevent it. I hope you understand that cheating says so much more about their character, than it does about yours. It often comes from a place of deep insecurity, selfishness, immaturity, or simply a lack of empathy for your feelings.

I think one of the hardest things following infidelity is deciding whether you should forgive them or let them go. It's an incredibly complicated situation to navigate, and everyone has different boundaries and tolerance levels, so what works for one person might not be the right decision for *you*. I made the choice to forgive an ex-boyfriend during my early twenties, for cheating multiple times. Partly because I was deeply in love with him. And partly because our relationship was long-term, and I had already invested a great deal of my time, heart, and energy into it. So, I felt that if I walked away then I would be losing the life I had worked so hard to build with him.

But sadly, the decision to forgive him became one of my biggest regrets – because our relationship *never* recovered. For months after, I was plagued day and night by the thought of him being intimate with someone else. It took a huge toll on my self-esteem, as I convinced myself that maybe I wasn't good enough for him, and that's why he decided to be unfaithful. Over time, I also started to resent him for his betrayal and breaking my trust beyond repair, but I hated myself even more for staying with him. I ultimately lost all respect for myself by ignoring my own boundaries.

So, if you are struggling to decide whether to forgive someone's infidelity, the question is not whether they are remorseful or deserve another chance. The real question is whether you can live with your choice to forgive them. Are you truly able to let it go, and find it in your heart to trust them again? And perhaps they are worthy of your forgiveness and second chances, but what are *you* worthy of?

This Is Not Love, It's Emotional Abuse

It took me the longest time to understand that there is a fine line between love and emotional abuse. That certain behaviours in a relationship can so easily be interpreted as affection, when in fact they are incredibly toxic. Love can be a powerful weapon, and abusive people are skilled at using love to keep the upper hand over you.

When I first started dating my ex, I thought the fact that he was in constant contact with me via texts and calls was an indicator of how much he liked me. That he closely checked and asked about my daily activities because he was genuinely interested in my life. But there is a fine between taking an interest in your day and *monitoring* your every move. This eventually leads to them wanting you to spend all your free time with them, and only them. Partly because of their *need* to control your every move, and partly because of their excessive jealousy.

Given that my previous relationship before him was built on infidelity and a lack of care, intense jealousy became incredibly attractive to me. I naively convinced myself that it was a sign of how deeply he loved me, and therefore would never disrespect my trust in the way that others had in the past. I think this was cemented in my mind even more by his justification – *"If I didn't love you then I wouldn't be so jealous."*

But while a small amount of jealousy in relationships is normal, healthy even, excessive and irrational jealousy can be incredibly emotionally abusive. There came a point where I was actively choosing to stay at home, avoid my friends, and stop making social plans that did not involve him. Because sacrificing my freedom became easier than dealing with his jealous behaviour.

And it does not stop there. Because if you start out by making small sacrifices to keep them happy, such as cancelling plans with friends, then how long will it be until you start to make much bigger and more significant sacrifices? If you find yourself giving up on your hopes and dreams because they react to them with contempt rather than kindness and support – then that's emotional abuse.

Please understand that if they condemn and oppose your life goals, it does not come from a place of love, or because they *'only want what is best'* for the both of you. It's most likely because those life changes could take you out of the realm of their control.

Emotional abusers are also skilled at eroding your self-esteem through subtle criticisms that they so easily disguise as loving complements. My ex would speak about how *lucky* I was that he 'chose me', given that he had his pick over numerous women. He would also frequently make comments like *"you're so beautiful, just a bit more work at the gym and you will be perfect"*, and *"you should take care of yourself more because you look amazing with make-up on."*

These types of comments are a confusion tactic, because words like 'beautiful' and 'amazing' can initially come across as a complement. But honestly, they are criticisms that are designed to slowly chip away at your confidence, so an abuser can gain even more control over you, as you start to believe that they are the only one who will ever accept and love you. I guess this notion became cemented in my belief system even more when my ex would constantly say *"nobody will ever love you like I do."*

Whenever I would question my ex about his backhanded complements, he would respond in an exasperated tone, saying that I was simply *"taking it the wrong way."* – something that I didn't recognise as gaslighting until much later, when I had already started to believe that *I* was the problem, and that maybe I was just too sensitive.

I think the deepest way that he used love as a weapon

in our relationship was with the *"if you love me, you will…"* – a powerful manipulation tactic. Because how could I ever say no, even when his demands crossed my boundaries, if doing so meant that I did not love him. It took me a long time to learn that you should never have to sacrifice yourself or do something you don't want to do just to *prove* your feelings to someone.

Cognitive Dissonance – The Belief Vs. The Reality

When you are deeply in love with someone, you build up a belief system about them that becomes almost impossible to fracture. In your mind, they are inherently good and moral, and would never do anything to hurt you or betray your trust. This is often why you choose to stay with the people who cause you pain, be it through infidelity or toxic behaviour, because your mind can't accept the reality of who they truly are.

Or rather, you don't *want* to believe the reality. Because when something conflicts with your internal beliefs, it creates intense feelings of discomfort. And so, you use cognitive dissonance as a coping mechanism to alleviate those feelings – by distorting the facts in your mind or simply overlook the truth. You undermine how toxic or hurtful their behaviour really is, even if the evidence is undeniable. You find ways to rationalise and justify their actions, because that's so much easier than changing your perception of them.

You love them so much that it's too painful to accept that they are not the person you thought they were. So, you frantically hold onto that perfect image of them with everything you have. You use this as justification for staying in the relationship, despite how deeply they continue to hurt you. But please understand that cognitive dissonance is a form of self-sabotage, and the longer you continue this cycle, the more damage it will cause.

The Truth About One-Sided Relationships

You deserve to be with someone who gives the same amount of care and love to you, as you give to them. Please don't drain yourself of your energy, time, support, and emotions, if you are receiving less than the bare minimum in return.

The truth is – you can't sustain a relationship alone. You shouldn't have to be the only one making the effort to spend time with them. You shouldn't have to feel like your emotional needs are being ignored. You shouldn't have to be the only one making sacrifices for the relationship to work. You shouldn't have to neglect everything else in your life because you're pouring all your energy into maintaining the relationship. You shouldn't always be questioning if they care about you. You shouldn't have to keep making excuses for their behaviour, for taking everything from you but giving you nothing meaningful in return.

Staying in a one-sided relationship is incredibly unhealthy, leaving you to feel an overwhelming sense of loneliness. One of the hardest things you will ever experience is sitting beside someone you love yet feeling more alone than ever, because they don't *see* you, so your emotional needs are constantly neglected.

If your continued efforts to communicate your feelings and needs are ignored, then it's time to walk away from the relationship for your own wellbeing, before it drains you of everything you have.

Alcohol And Abusive Relationships

When you are deeply in love with someone who has an unhealthy relationship with alcohol, I think it becomes custom to blame their toxic behaviour on that substance. But one of the hardest realities I had to face in an abusive relationship, is that alcohol does not *cause* someone to be abusive towards you.

Truthfully, there is a positive correlation between alcohol consumption and domestic abuse, but not so much a *causality*. Meaning that alcohol exacerbates the abuse that was already there. It lowers an abuser's inhibitions enough to allow that behaviour to rise to the surface, from whatever deep place they keep it hidden. It also gives them the confidence to treat you in that way without consciously thinking about the consequences. Put simply – alcohol adds *fuel* to the fire.

It took years of therapy, and deep diving into my own psychology background to fully understand and accept this revelation. I guess it was easier for me to believe that alcohol was the sole cause of my ex's abusive behaviour, than to acknowledge how deeply those toxic traits ran within him. I guess it was easier to entertain the lies that the way he treated me was a mistake, that it would never happen again, and that the alcohol simply made him 'lose control'.

The truth is, he was *always* in control. In every setting where alcohol was involved, he was easily able to act in a perfectly normal way towards others. Friends, family, and even strangers. I was the exception. Yet he would still try to convince me afterwards that he didn't mean to hurt me, it was *only* because he was drunk, he lost control and didn't know what he was doing – or even remember what he had done. But truthfully, it was easier for him to say that he did not remember, because that way he didn't have to take responsibility for his actions, or admit that he was an abuser.

One of the most profound parts of my healing journey was when my therapist asked me "does he treat his mother or sister in the same awful way when he's been drinking?", and I replied "no, of course not, he adores them". This highlighted the point in the most painful but incredible way – that my ex was still completely aware of his actions, because if he wasn't then he would most likely be abusive to everyone around him. The fact that he was still kind and caring towards others meant that his abusive behaviour towards me was a *choice*.

Who Are They, Really?

Sometimes, two versions exist of the person you love. One version is affectionate, kind and leaves you feeling euphoric. And the other version is cold, heartless and leaves you feeling dejected. They seem to switch between the two so interchangeably that you are left feeling confused, and anxiously anticipating which side of the coin you will endure that day.

So, you ask yourself repeatedly, who are they *really?*

The painfully honest answer is that only one version of them is real – the one they become when their mask slips. The other is a lie, just a perfectly crafted façade they show to the world, a mask they want people to believe is their true face.

But eventually, cracks begin to appear, and you witness the ugliness within. This is not some beautiful caterpillar into a butterfly transformation, no. This is a toxic transformation.

I've learned that people often do show you who they truly are, from the very beginning. Even in the subtlest of ways. Although, you choose to ignore it, either consciously or subconsciously. You *want* to believe the lie, because that version of them is everything you ever dreamed of. But from what I know of heartbreak – when someone shows you who they *really* are, it's better to believe them the first time.

Please Leave Before You Lose Yourself

I hope you find the strength to walk away from a toxic relationship before you lose yourself. Before it destroys every fibre that makes you, *you*. Before you no longer recognise the person staring back at you in the mirror.

I know it's incredibly hard to do this, when you're not even aware that you're losing yourself in the relationship until the damage has already taken hold. It begins slowly, by sacrificing yourself in small ways to keep your partner happy and maintain the relationship. Then over time, this develops into a much deeper pattern of sacrifice. Before you know it, you're cutting off friends or family, giving up your goals and dreams, and forgiving behaviours that completely go against your boundaries.

As the toxicity of the relationship continues to build, you slowly feel yourself fading away, becoming a shadow of the person you used to be. And the most heart-breaking thing about this, is that you blame yourself. You feel guilt, anger and resentment for allowing your self-esteem, self-respect and autonomy to be diminished by the person you gave your heart to. Something that you could never imagine allowing to happen before you met them.

Towards the end of my relationship with my ex, I felt completely lost, because I realised that I had become unrecognisable in every sense. Mentally, physically and emotionally. The light that used to radiate from me had been entirely dimmed. Slowly giving up my freedom and choices for the one I loved had turned me into a shell of a person. Someone who was overwhelmed with anxiety, depression, hopelessness and despair. Because of this, my mind and body became numb, as though it was in a daze, or a state of shock. And it wasn't until after the breakup that I was able to fully comprehend the damage the relationship had caused – like waking up from a nightmare and assessing my surroundings to see what was real.

Please understand that sometimes walking away from someone you love is the only option. I know you maybe don't want to right now, but you *need* to – to save yourself before it destroys every beautiful thing you are.

This Is How It Feels to Have Your Heart Broken (By Someone You Thought Was Your Soulmate)

Someone once told me that having your heart broken can feel like grieving a person who is still alive – and they were *right*.

In those initial days and weeks after the breakup, the pain is so intense and overwhelming that you truly believe you won't survive it. In those moments, the whole world feels like it's crashing down around you, an explosion of your reality.

You watch everything go up in flames – the life you built together, your plans and hopes for the future, the comfort of the stability and the *known*. Yet, there is nothing you can do to stop it.

The hurt is so profound that it feels as though it's burning you from the inside out, emotional pain becoming physical pain. Your chest physically aches, the pain constricting your lungs with each inhale. Your stomach feels like it's twisted in knots, waves of nausea hitting you every time you think of *them*.

Each day you function on autopilot because your mind is so consumed by the breakup, leaving little mental capacity for anything else. Sleep becomes your only reprieve from the hurt, but it's bittersweet, because once you wake up, you're hit with a fresh wave of pain by remembering and acknowledging your new reality – as though you're living a waking nightmare.

The reason it hurts so much is because when you love someone, they come to live in the emotional centre of your brain, physically occupying the neurons. So, your brain gets confused after a breakup, as it still *expects* to see them – to touch them, hear them, and feel them. And when you can no longer do that, the emotional centre of your brain becomes inflamed by desperately searching for them, leading to emotional and even *physical* pain.

I know right now the heartbreak is so physically and emotionally exhausting, that you can't imagine a time when you won't feel this way. But please understand that everything you feel in this moment is *temporary*. Emotions are a fluid part of the human experience, reflecting only how you feel right now. I know it's an incredibly hard lesson to learn, but you will *not* die from a broken heart.

Right now you can't imagine ever being okay with their

absence from your life – but you *will*. Right now you can't imagine a day where it doesn't feel like your heart is being ripped from your chest – but that day *will* come. Right now you can only see what you are losing, and not what you will gain – but soon you *will* understand. Right now you are so deep in rock bottom that it feels like you will never get back up again – but you *will* rise stronger than ever before.

How Defence Mechanisms Can Sabotage Your Relationship

It's human nature to use defence mechanisms to protect us from our worst fears and anxieties – we are hardwired to unconsciously respond to perceived threats in a defensive way, to promote our *survival*.

But those same defence mechanisms we use for self-protection can sometimes do more harm than good, especially when it comes to relationships. Because of the deep and intense emotions we experience, our coping mechanisms can become maladaptive, leading to self-sabotaging behaviours – which ultimately damage our relationship in the process.

Denial became my failsafe in my last relationship. I spent years ignoring toxic behaviours, and convinced myself that everything would work out between us, without ever properly addressing the underlying problems we had. I think I also knew, deep in my soul, that the relationship was not right for me, that *he* was not right for me – but still, I lived in a state of denial for the longest time. I guess it was easier in that moment to ignore the issues, a way of avoiding the pain and conflict that would come with acknowledging the reality. But more than that, I now understand that it was a way for me to hold on to the relationship, when I really needed to let go.

Those toxic behaviours I was in denial of, were a by-product of my ex-partners own defence mechanisms. *Displacement* and *compensation* became his failsafe's during our relationship. For every bad day he had, every stressful situation he encountered, every person who frustrated him – the anger that consumed him was always displaced onto me. I became nothing more than his emotional punching bag. His lack of emotional maturity also had him turning to alcohol as a coping mechanism, a way to compensate his negative emotions. It became easier for him to reach for a drink, than to confront his emotions, or communicate with me about what was bothering him.

The turbulent nature of our relationship then had me resorting back to my default coping mechanism – building *defensive walls*. Around myself, around my emotions, and around my heart. This behaviour first took form in my early childhood, where I developed a deep-rooted fear of abandonment due to trauma and poor attachments. Then through unhealthy adult relationships, the need to build protective barriers around myself grew exponentially. In my unconscious mind, my first reaction was to pull away from people who got too close, a perceived '*safe distance*' – a way to protect myself from any further potential pain and heartbreak. When in reality, I was only sabotaging myself and my relationship by acting in a cold and detached manner – closing my heart to the beauty of love, and not only the pain.

Poisonous Love

One of the hardest lessons I ever had to learn, was that love can be a *poison*.

It did not start off that way. In its natural form, love is wholly good, pure, and true. But through endless conflicts, possessiveness, unrealistic expectations, insecurities and co-dependency, it was twisted into something toxic.

The wholesome and affectionate love we once shared became a poison – to *both* of our souls. For me, it made me accept unhealthy behaviour that was slowly tearing me apart. I had only ever experienced love in half measures in the past, so I romanticised the idea of an all-consuming love.

For him, it took away all rational thought and logic. He described himself as being 'crazy and madly in love', which caused him act in a way that he wouldn't ordinarily. Behaviour that he knew, deep down, was incredibly toxic.

For both of us, the excessive amount of love we held

for each other created a tunnel vision – leading us to react in improper ways. The very love that bound our hearts became the rationality for holding onto the toxic relationship. We rarely stopped to consider the poisonous consequences; we were solely guided by our intense emotions.

I guess my insecurities loved the fact that I never had to question his feelings for me. There was never a doubt in my mind whether he loved me or not – that was not the problem. The downfall of our relationship was because of *how much* he loved me, and me him. The love consumed us, and ripped us apart in the process.

It Is Not Your Job to Change
or Fix Someone

The most toxic thing I have ever done, is convince myself that I can fix someone. That if I loved him deeply enough then he would change his cruel behaviour, *for me*. That if I could somehow show him that I'm worthy of his affection, then he would *want* to treat me better.

If I'm honest with myself, the red flags were there from the very beginning of our relationship – huge neon warning signs screaming at me from every direction. But I still let him into my life, and my heart, because I chose to only see the good parts of him. I romanticised what the relationship *could* be, and who he could be, rather than seeing things as they truly were.

When I finally had no choice but to acknowledge his red flags, I naively thought that I could change him, by loving him deeply and fiercely. As if my love and dedication alone would be enough to spark that transformation within him. That hope burned in me for four long and tumultuous years. Waiting and waiting for a change that was never to come.

In that time, I somehow ended up in a scenario where all my time and energy were spent trying to unpick every toxic behaviour he exhibited, to try and find some root cause, so that I could help him to heal. Then maybe, just maybe, I could continue loving him without getting burned. But the fact that I was searching for reasons to explain the red flags were a part of the problem, because those so-called reasons became *excuses*. So, through every failed attempt to change his toxic habits, he and I would both rationalise his behaviour due to his past experiences.

I wish I knew then, what I know now – that you can't change someone who doesn't want to change for themselves. And more than that, you can't fix behaviours that they don't even recognise as being hurtful.

The truth is, it is not your responsibility to *fix* someone. It is not your job to try and save them from their own toxic habits, no matter how much you love them. You can love and support them through their issues, but if they don't show up for their own healing and growth, you can't do it for them. Giving your life and energy to try and change them will only result in you hurting and destroying yourself. Please remember that you were not placed on this earth just to be someone else's emotional crutch, or worse, their *emotional punching bag*.

Emotional Abuse and The Lasting Scars

I think the danger of emotional abuse is that it's not always so outwardly obvious. It can sometimes be subtle, hidden behind sweet words and gestures, which makes it incredibly hard to recognise – until the damage has already started to take hold. Like a darkness slowly seeping into your mind, contaminating your self-image, self-esteem, and mental health.

As I tried to heal from a relationship that was both physically and emotionally abusive, I kind of believed that the physical scars would be much harder to heal than the emotional ones. Because the physical bruises and scars were *visible*, right on the surface where I could see them daily. But I soon came to realise that the emotional wounds ran so much deeper than I could have ever imagined. I guess the fact that they were internal, invisible to the naked eye, just made it harder to truly comprehend the profound impact they had left on my mind, my heart, and my soul.

In the immediate aftermath of the breakup, I was spiralling in self-doubt. I guess when you have been criticised and gaslighted for so long by someone you deeply love, you eventually believe that everything they say is the truth. So, you're left feeling overwhelmingly confused, questioning whether the relationship was truly *that* bad, and whether you were the cause of its downfall. This goes hand in hand with the low self-esteem that consumed me, because how could I possibly find any shred of good in myself, when all I'd heard for four long years was that I was *nothing*. Too sensitive, too damaged, too difficult to love. Subsequently, I isolated myself from every other person I loved out of fear that they would have the same criticisms of me too, cementing the idea that I was wholly unworthy.

But sadly, the long-term emotional wounds were so much more profound, especially since the emotional abuse had been a slow burn over a long period of time. Slowly smouldering in my mind, no flames or smoke to warn me of the internal damage.

It wasn't until after the breakup that I realised my mental health had become a pile of ash, teeming with depression and anxiety. And I was left to desperately try to repair myself, through months of therapy and medication. On the outside I was numb, completely uninterested in anything that used to bring me joy. But on the inside, I was drowning in sadness, and I couldn't remember what happiness or mental peace felt like.

Every day was a battle to get out of bed and try to continue living.

But I think the deepest emotional wound I was left with, the one that took the longest to heal, was the fear of opening my heart to someone else. My emotional walls became my biggest defence mechanism, and it was so much easier for me to remain cold and detached, than to trust another person that could potentially hurt me. No matter how much I wanted or *needed* a connection, I just couldn't let anyone break past the fortress I'd built around my heart.

I'm slowly learning that these emotional wounds, just like the physical ones, might always have some form of presence. I sometimes catch a glance of a physical scar on my wrist, inflicted by him the night we broke up. It's now faded into two silver lines, but still very much evident. A visual reminder of the suffering I endured, but also a remembrance of what I escaped. I'm slowly learning that this scar mirrors my emotional healing – if the physical scars still linger, then how can I expect the emotional wounds not to?

So maybe there is a piece of my soul, deep down, that is forever changed from the trauma of the relationship. *And that's okay.* I am slowly learning to wear all my scars with pride, a reminder of my courage and strength.

An Apology Without Change
Is Manipulation

I think it's even harder to break free from a toxic person when you're always met with *seemingly* heartfelt apologies and fresh promises, whenever they do something that causes you pain. If you are feeling stuck in the cycle of a toxic relationship right now, I want you to know something I wish I would have learned sooner – an apology without change is manipulation.

A true and sincere apology involves recognising the harmful impact of your actions, showing remorse, and having the desire to not repeat them in the future. So, if you keep hearing apology after apology but nothing ever changes, then their behaviour is a conscious *choice*, and something they don't ever intend to change.

I hope you begin to understand that those apologies and promises are just empty words, an emotional manipulation tactic that toxic people use to keep you hooked on them. They tell you what you want to hear, simply to make you feel better about the situation without doing anything to change it.

Numbing Your Heartache

Sometimes the pain of heartbreak is so profound that it becomes too much to bear. So much so, that you would do anything to *not* feel it. Sometimes heartbreak is so overwhelming that you desperately search for some magical button that will allow you to switch off your feelings.

You know that being in a state of numbness is no way to live, but becoming emotionless to everything around you seems like the better alternative to enduring such shattering heartache. So, you continue to suppress your emotions, burying them in the deepest depths of your subconscious. Believing that the more hidden they are, the less power they have to hurt you.

But numbing your heartache does not mean that it's suddenly gone, miraculously healed overnight – it's just buried under the surface of your consciousness. Slowly eating away at you, screaming to be let out. I hope you know that suppressing your emotions will only sabotage your healing, because you cannot heal what you refuse to let yourself *feel*. And so, you become trapped in a cycle with that unresolved pain, never being able to truly move on.

I know it's sometimes easier said than done, allowing yourself to sit with the hurt, to listen to it, to embrace it rather than run from it. Because the thing is, from an evolutionary perspective we are hardwired to see everything in nature as good or bad. So your first instinct following a breakup is to try to make yourself feel better as swiftly as possible, to protect your heart and mind from emotions that you consider to be 'bad' – pain, guilt, anger or grief. But I want you to know that emotions are not wholly good or bad, they simply *are*. I hope that by removing this judgment, you are able to truly feel and accept every emotion that comes with heartbreak, without fear or avoidance.

Please remember, that no matter how much your heart seems to be breaking right now, these painful feelings will *not* kill you. Emotions are a temporary and fluid part of the human experience, simply reflecting how you currently feel. They will only stick around longer than necessary if you don't process them and find a healthy outlet. Please, let yourself feel, then let it go.

The Cycle of Self-Sabotage

Going back to the person who tore your heart out is like walking head on into traffic and expecting not to get hurt. You *know*, deep down, that it's not good for you. Still, you find yourself repeating the same toxic cycle again and again.

But please understand that the more chances you give them, the less respect they will have for you – and the more you will lose respect for yourself in the process. They won't ever be afraid of losing you, as they know that whatever they do you will always welcome them back with open arms.

I know this, because I kept doing it – for *years*. And each time I went back, the more I loathed myself.

I've come to learn that persistently going back to an unhealthy relationship is a form of self-sabotage, often stemming from *self-doubt*. So, the one who caused us deep pain becomes the one we believe can make us feel better, to provide that sense of reassurance and acceptance we deeply crave. This is even more prevalent when the relationship was toxic and had eroded our identity and self-esteem over a long period of time.

I hope as you heal, you learn that you are whole and worthy without them. I hope as you heal, you begin to remember who you are. To find your strength. To remember your value and worthiness. To take control of your own needs and desires. To break that self-sabotaging cycle of going back to the one you *know* is not good for you.

The Familiarity of Toxic Relationships

If you gather the fragments of my dating and relationship history, from my teenage years to my late twenties, you will see a blaring common feature throughout – *toxicity*.

As I worked on my healing following my last breakup, I finally started to question why I often found myself gravitating towards toxic people. There had to be some common denominator, perhaps my judgement or decision-making, that repeatedly pulled me towards unhealthy relationships – as though I purposely sought them out, as though I *enjoyed* the pain they inflicted…

…and that is not so far from the reality. The uncomfortable truth is that for most of my adult life, I have been subconsciously seeking the *comfort* of toxic relationships – because they are all I have ever known.

Our earliest relationships, that we either experience or witness, subsequently become the blueprint for all future relationships. So, for those of us who have lived through any type of trauma, chaos or toxicity – the unhealthy features of those relationships eventually become normalised. We start to consider unsupportive behaviour, intense anger, or extreme fights as a normal part of adult relationships. They don't deter us like they should, rather, they draw us in – because of the comfort we find in the *familiarity*.

This completely distorted my sense of what a healthy relationship should look like, and *feel* like. I associated toxic behaviours with an intense expression of love. I considered raging arguments to be a normal method of communication. I found comfort in the chaos, because at least I knew what to expect there. The familiarity of the pain felt like *safety* to me.

Because of this, any relationship that differed from my norm felt incredibly uncomfortable, triggering even. When you have only ever known an unhealthy type of love, healthy relationships seem wholly wrong. And the peace starts to look like boredom.

This was an incredibly hard realisation to have – that I have rejected people in the past simply because of my unfamiliarity with the *peace*. And it was this lack of familiarity that caused me deep feelings of discomfort and anxiety, *not* because the relationship was lacking or wrong as I previously believed.

The sad truth is, for some of us, the chaos and toxicity is our comfort zone. So, stepping into a stable, peaceful and loving relationship means stepping out of our comfort zone and into the unknown – an incredibly scary feat. But, as I heal my inner child, I am slowly learning to love what is *good* for me.

The Bare Minimum

It took me a long time to realise that the *highs* we so desperately crave in toxic relationships are not highs at all. Not really.

The sad truth is, when you regularly experience such poor treatment, the things you consider to be highs and lows are distorted. Constantly crying becomes normal, familiar even. And those brief moments of not being made to feel like human trash feel like ecstasy.

In my last relationship, I lived through what I can only describe as a toxic abyss. For years, it was a daily pattern of fights, jealousy, control, and verbal abuse. So, something as normal as being treated with kindness and respect, or a simple display of affection – well, they began to feel like *nirvana*. Because the less I experienced affection, the rarer and more special it became.

I craved what I believed were euphoric moments with him. Truthfully, they were just the bare minimum treatment I deserved from the one I entrusted with the entirety of my heart.

Not Healed, Just Numb

I thought I had got better at dealing with heartbreak. As though the deeper the pain I experienced, the more resilient I became. Like a skill that could be mastered with endless practice. The truth is, there is a fine line between emotional intelligence and emotional *numbness*.

I thought I was mostly unscathed after my last painful breakup. Only shedding a few small tears, nothing like the gut wrenching sobs I'd endured in the aftermath of past breakups. I seemed to swiftly continue with my life as normal, like those years I'd spent with someone I'd considered to be the love of my life never even happened.

But how could that be? The intensity of that relationship, along with how badly it ended, was so much worse than any breakup I'd ever experienced. I still remember the feelings of absolute devastation after things ended with my first long-term boyfriend at 23. So, I couldn't comprehend why I didn't feel like that now, despite knowing that I'd loved so much deeper and harder this time around.

For the longest time, I told myself that this was a good thing. Congratulated myself, even. Fully convinced that I'd become so emotionally resilient that I was just able to move on from heartache without a second thought.

It took me more than six months after the breakup to realise that my emotional intelligence was not responsible for my lack of sadness – because I wasn't healed, not in the slightest. I was completely *numb*, void of all feelings.

It was as though I had experienced and expressed so many painful emotions during the relationship that I was now depleted, and had no emotions left inside of me. The days passed me by in a blur, my body functioning on autopilot whilst my mind was fully checked out.

And that's the difficulty when a relationship or breakup is so traumatic, your mind subconsciously tries to bury those painful feelings below the surface, out of reach – a method of self-protection.

In my case, the trauma and loss were so profound that my mind had rapidly and messily stuck a bandage over the wound, without treating or caring for it.

But it could never heal like that, so I eventually had to make the conscious decision to tear open the wound, let it breathe, and allow all those repressed emotions to pour out. As painful as it may be, feeling everything at once is better than feeling nothing at all.

How Childhood Attachments Can Affect Adult Relationships

It's human nature to seek love, connection and support in others. We have this deep and innate *need* to belong. So, forming an attachment to someone you love can be a beautiful thing; after all, it is a representation of the emotional bond you have created. But, developing an unhealthy attachment style can cause us a great deal of pain and suffering in relationships.

For those of us with attachment issues, we often find ourselves stuck in a cycle of unhealthy or emotionally draining patterns in our romantic relationships. And the sad truth is, these attachment issues can almost always be traced back to our childhood experiences.

The earliest bonds we form as children become the blueprint for the relationships we have throughout our adult lives, they create an internal model of what we *think* relationships should be like.

So, if we experienced the love and care we needed in childhood, then we feel secure and *safe* when becoming attached to our partners later in life. But, if we were deprived of secure attachments during those early years, we will subsequently feel insecure, afraid, or anxious in our attachments throughout adulthood – because our unconscious mind believes, and *expects*, that every person we ever love will treat us with the same lack of care we endured in childhood.

It wasn't until I reached my mid-twenties, and spent countless hours in gruelling therapy sessions, that I began to fully understand the lasting impact of the first few years of my life. In the days after I was brought into this world, I was given up for adoption. It was absolutely the right decision for my biological mother to make, for both of our well-beings; but, that also meant that I spent the first year of my life in the foster care system. Because of this, I never really developed those crucial child-caregiver bonds – not in a healthy way, anyway.

I've heard stories told with humour, of the time after I was adopted, where I would uncontrollably sob and scream whenever my parents would leave the room – or if they even moved in a way that appeared as though they were about to up and leave me. But now, as an adult, I find that story incredibly sad. Because I understand that it's the behaviour of a young child who had a crushing fear of *abandonment*.

It still feels so strange to me, that I have absolutely no recollection of the first few years of my life, only photographs and stories. Yet, I know it's had such a profound impact on who I am today – particularly, the way I experience romantic connections. On the surface, I come across as incredibly independent, and emotionally resilient. But, underneath that, I have a deep-rooted fear of abandonment and rejection – which are typical features of an anxious attachment.

In every adult relationship I've experienced, I subconsciously believed that they would eventually break my heart and then walk out of my life. The fear of abandonment was so innate, that it did not matter how many promises they made, or how much love and care they showed me, I just couldn't trust them – there was *always* a small part of my mind that was waiting for their rejection.

Because of this, I often felt incredibly anxious in the relationship, which would then influence my behaviour towards them. I would question their feelings for me, place them on an incredibly high pedestal and convince myself I wasn't good enough for them, rely on them for validation to boost my self-esteem, and overanalyse conversations and text messages – believing even the slightest change in their tone meant that they were angry with me, because maybe I said or did something wrong. I rarely even questioned if *they* were right for *me*, I was too focused on keeping them in my life purely out of fear.

The fear of abandonment and rejection was most crippling during my teenage years and early twenties, intensified by my biological father's refusal to acknowledge my existence when I attempted to reach out to him the moment I turned eighteen – which hurt so much worse than his initial rejection when I was a child. In my subconscious, this solidified the idea that everyone I ever love will eventually reject and abandon me.

So, it's maybe not surprising that I am often drawn to toxic or emotionally unavailable men in adulthood. Because, when we have unresolved trauma from childhood relationships, we sometimes unconsciously recreate similar relationship dynamics in adulthood. This has some biological underpinnings – our earliest attachments are registered by our nervous system as being the norm in relationships. So, if you received love and validation from a parent figure as a child, then you would typically avoid toxic, chaotic or neglectful relationships later in life. If not, it can feel *safer* or more comfortable to attach yourself to people who display neither of those things.

The sad truth is, we unknowingly repeat what we don't heal, and will continue to do so until we heal any underlying trauma from our childhood, and realise that we are *worthy* of a healthy love.

Although somewhat innate, attachment styles don't

necessarily stay the same throughout our entire lives. So, if you struggle with an anxious attachment in romantic relationships, it *is* possible to overcome it – by first making the intentional effort to understand your attachment style. It's important to deeply make sense of how you interact in romantic relationships, and *why*. Once you have this self-awareness, you will then be able to foster new patterns of thinking, and develop healthier habits in your relationships.

But, it's also incredibly important *who* you choose to attach yourself to. Because, if you choose a partner who is toxic or emotionally unavailable, then this will only increase the anxiety in your attachment to them. The relationship will likely be chaotic, confusing and painful. Whereas, if you choose to be with a partner who is supportive, stable, and loving, they can help to shift you away from the negative thought patterns that come with an anxious attachment. The love and care that they outwardly show will also play an important role in building your sense of security in the relationship.

You Know When It's Not Right (Even If You Don't Want to Admit It)

Sometimes it deeply frustrates me, looking back on my first long-term relationship. To acknowledge how much of my life I shared with someone that I *knew* was not right for me, years before it was over. I felt it, with every fibre of my being, that it was not meant to last – yet I chose to ignore my intuition.

There were nights where I would lay awake beside him, restless and unable to sleep – because I had an overwhelming sense that something was *wrong*. Some nights the sensation was so intense that I fell into a panic, the walls closing in on me at the thought of this being my life forever.

Yet I still held onto the relationship with everything I had, desperately convincing myself that nothing was wrong, and I was just overthinking it.

But the truth is, you can lie to your mind, but you can't lie to your soul. When something or someone is not right for you, you will *feel* it right down in the pit of your stomach, a nagging feeling that you can't seem to shake off. Whenever you are around them, you're plagued with a deep sense of unease – your soul's way of warning you that the relationship is not right for you. And the more you ignore that feeling, the more intense it becomes.

For me, the hardest part was trying to distinguish what was my intuition and what was my anxiety. Because I had struggled with intense anxiety for so many years, I was sure that my intuition could not be trusted anymore.

And so, I fell into a cycle of ignoring every gut feeling I had – even when they screamed at me from within. But on some level, I think my anxiety just became the perfect excuse, a reason to ignore everything I knew to be true about the relationship but did not want to accept.

Even if you do struggle with anxiety, I have come to understand that the sense of knowing you have about someone – your gut feeling – should *always* be listened to.

Because truthfully, if you feel deeply anxious and not at ease when spending time with someone, know that it's because they are not right for you, and the anxiety is your bodies way of reminding you of this. Know that everything that is right for you will give you a deep sense of peace.

So please, trust that your soul knows what is good for you, even when your heart is being stubborn. And when your soul tries to warn you that something is wrong, *let it go*.

PART TWO:

resurfacing

Resurfacing [*n*.]: to rise and come back up to the surface; reform or reappear after a period of time.

A Failed Relationship Is
Not a Failure

We live in a society that has led us to believe that breakups are failures, and *only* relationship continuity equates to success. We've internalised this idea so deeply that we consider anything less than a lifelong commitment to be a complete waste of our time.

Our very biology makes it all the more difficult to challenge this idea. We are wired to create and maintain attachments; so, when we commit our hearts to someone, our nervous system tells us that the relationship is supposed to last forever. After a breakup, that same nervous system then triggers self-doubt – that *we* are a failure because we couldn't make the relationship last.

But, I want you to know that a failed love is *not* a failure in life. Every love, and every heartbreak, helped shape you into the person you are today. You just need to shift your focus from the loss, to what you ultimately learned and gained.

The truth is, every time you gave your heart to someone, you also seized the opportunity to practice *vulnerability*. You risked your heart, in the hopes of finding the love that you deserve. Even in the face of potential loss and pain, you still chose to keep your heart open, and allowed yourself to be vulnerable with someone – an incredibly beautiful and *strong* thing to do, in this harsh dating culture.

Even if this ultimately resulted in heartbreak, it was *not* a failure. And it was not a waste of your time or effort. Every single heartbreak is a new opportunity for growth and self-development. It gives you the space to take a step back and think about what you truly want, in life and in love. You are able to reflect on what you liked or didn't like about your last relationship, what your communication style and love language is, what your boundaries and needs are, and what you liked or didn't like about *yourself* in the relationship. This perspective is a huge win, not only for getting to know yourself on a deeper level, but also using this knowledge to choose more wisely in the future – of who deserves to hold your heart.

The Purpose of The Pain

Heartbreak, like all other pain, is crucial for human growth. It's the *resistance* to that hurt that causes us to suffer.

From a simple evolutionary perspective, pain teaches us what is good for us within our environment, and what is not. But beyond evolution, heartbreak is also crucial for the growth of our minds, our hearts, and our souls.

The pain of heartbreak is often a catalyst that breaks us open, in order to rebuild as the stronger and more beautiful being we were always meant to become. Reaching rock bottom feels like a breakdown, when it's actually a *breakthrough*.

It forces us to leave behind what was comfortable and build a life that is authentically ours. To let go of what was always meant to be lost and make space for what was destined to be gained.

The truth is, you *will* feel pain, you will feel sorrow, and you will feel loss – that's a part of the human experience. But please understand that pain is not the enemy, it is there to help you grow into the person you are meant to be. So embrace the ugliness of heartbreak, don't resist the pain, listen to it, *feel* it, allow it to transform you.

Rejection Is Not a Reflection of Your Worth

From as early as I can remember, I grew into the habit of internalising romantic rejection, viewing it as a sign of my unworthiness. My mind never responded with '*I deserve better*', instead, it screamed '*I'm not good enough*'.

I allowed rejection to wholly dictate my self-worth, and let it drag me into a pit of self-loathing. I would pick myself apart – physically, mentally and behaviourally, desperately trying to change the parts that I perceived to be inadequacies. Shaping myself into something that was less *me*, but what I thought would be more desirable to others.

It took me years of therapy and gruelling inner work to realise that the root issue was my low self-esteem, and not so much the rejection itself.

The truth is, having a healthy level of self-esteem can serve as a kind of 'buffer' to rejection, absorbing some of the shock and hurt that comes along with it. Although, rejection for those of us with poor self-esteem can trigger the fight-or-flight response, because the *fear* of rejection runs much deeper within us – right into our very core.

This causes us to respond to rejection in a more vulnerable and defensive way, whilst hindering our ability to see it in a true and rational context. And so, the feeling of being rejected by someone we allowed into our heart is utterly soul crushing. We become convinced that we're simply not worthy of being loved and accepted by others, and *never* will be – internalising the rejection so deeply that it forces us to reject ourselves in the process.

But I want you to know something, a fact that helped me to process rejection in a much healthier way – the rejection is more about *them*, and less about you. Their inability to see your value is a reflection of them, and not a reflection of your worth.

It was also incredibly helpful for me, and I hope for you too, to understand that rejection is simply a form of *redirection* from something that wasn't good for you. Because if they were able to walk away from the relationship so easily, then they were *not* the right person for you. And sometimes it's hard to recognise that when your heart aches from the sting of rejection, or to notice their red flags when you're too busy picking yourself apart and doubting your worth.

I hope you remember that rejection is the universe's way of redirecting you towards something better, towards *someone* better. Someone who will see your value, and appreciate everything that you are. Someone who is truly worthy of your time, energy and love.

Why We Repeat The Same Unhealthy Relationship Patterns

It wasn't until I reached my late twenties, that I began to notice unhealthy patterns in my dating and relationship history, stretching all the way back to my teenage years. Each experience, although different, had similar underlying patterns – similar issues, similar fights, similar toxic behaviours.

The truth is, it's in our human nature to be driven by habits. We are drawn to what is familiar, what is *comfortable*. And so, we sometimes find ourselves repeating the same unhealthy or destructive relationship patterns, often unintentionally – through a string of subconscious choices.

Sometimes, we repeat unhealthy relationship patterns because we did not fix the underlying problems in our previous relationships – such as trust issues, jealousy, unmet needs, or even some type of trauma. And so, we end up projecting them onto our new partner. Deep trust issues became a defining part of my last relationship, leading to toxic behaviours and fights. We grew into the habit of comparing each other to our previous partners, becoming convinced that we would eventually be betrayed in the same way. It took me a long time to understand that people often repeat what they don't *repair*. We had both experienced situations in the past that destroyed the trust we held for someone we loved – but we never fully processed our feelings afterwards, or healed our hearts enough to be able to trust someone again.

Sometimes, we repeat unhealthy relationship patterns because we continually stick to a specific *'type'* of person to date, rather than remaining open to people who are different from our previous experiences – who might ultimately be more *right* for us in the long-term. Instead, we become attached to certain personalities, physical characteristics, or even people who are emotionally unavailable.

Sometimes, we repeat unhealthy relationship patterns because we are desperately hoping for a different outcome – particularly when returning to a toxic relationship we already tried to walk away from. We think that if we act even kinder, try even harder, find the right words or behaviour to please them, then this time it will work out. This time they will shows us the affection and acceptance we crave. But you may be familiar with this famous quote by Albert Einstein – *"the definition of insanity is doing the same thing over and over again but expecting different results*". Hence to say, we can't keep getting tangled up in the same destructive relationship and expect any other outcome than a broken heart and a shattered sense of self-worth.

Sometimes, we repeat unhealthy relationship patterns because we rapidly jump from one relationship to another – usually to avoid a deep fear of being *alone*. But that time spent alone, outside of any romantic relationship, is crucial for self-reflection. To process our feelings, to learn from our past mistakes, to understand what we deserve; and above all, to heal our heart before giving it to someone else.

Love And Hate - Two Sides of The Same Coin

When you are trying to heal from a broken heart, I know you might think that hating the one who hurt you is easiest way to move on. Maybe you believe that to hate them is the only way to let go of the intense love you felt.

But truthfully, there is a fine line between love and hate – they are two sides of the same coin.

Just like love, hate is a powerful emotion. So, keeping that hate in your heart means that you are still holding onto strong feelings for the one you are desperately trying to get over. And for as long as you hold those deep feelings, it will keep you tied to them.

Please understand that hate is not the opposite of love – it's *indifference*. To be indifferent is to let go of all the emotions you once held for them, love, hate, care, anger. All of them. It's to reach a state of neutrality where they are concerned, the only way to set your heart free and *truly* move on from them.

I know this is easier said than done, when it feels so much easier to hate them for all they put you through. But I hope with time, you learn to take those strong emotions you're desperately holding onto and direct them back to yourself – into your passions, into your goals, into loving yourself in the way that you deserve after so much loss.

Love Is an Elemental Force
of Nature

When it's over, you are left wondering *'where does the love go?'*

When it's over, I know it can feel like a profound loss. You spent so many months, maybe even years, pouring all of your love into a relationship – only for it to end. You're left feeling empty. That they drained all of the love you held in your heart, and took it with them as they left. That your love was wasted on someone who did not deserve it, and now it's lost forever. That you will never find enough love in your heart again to love someone else; or worse, to love yourself.

The beautiful thing is, love is an elemental force of nature, just like gravity or electromagnetism. In this way, love is *uncontainable*. So, no matter how much love you pour into a relationship, it won't be contained there forever. When it's over, that love will transcend, and find its way back to where it belongs – within you.

I know you feel completely empty and drained right now, but please know that love can be nurtured and channelled, but it can't be killed or lost. Just like gravity pulls all matter towards the centre of the earth, love will always be drawn back into your heart. No matter what blocks arise, it will *always* find its way.

You Won't Be Too Much for The Right Person

One of the hardest parts my healing journey, was trying to find my way back to myself. I had spent the entirety of my twenties moulding myself into something that wasn't *truly* me, trying to fit into a constricted box that each relationship had placed around me. Just to make them happy. Just to be loved. Just to be accepted. Just to hold onto someone who was not right for me.

I grew into the habit of changing certain parts of myself in a relationship, so I could meet their needs and seamlessly fit into their life without conflict. My desires, my expectations, my boundaries, even my emotional reactions. Over time, I became a lost piece of a puzzle, shaving off parts of who I was just to fit into a picture that was never meant for me.

And that's the danger of loving the wrong person, no matter what you do and who you become, you will never be *enough* for them.

I had never felt as hard to love as I did in my last relationship. If I openly expressed my emotions, then

I was too emotional. If I controlled my feelings and emotional reactions, then I was too cold. If I expressed the struggles I had with my mental health, then I was too weak. If I acted as though nothing ever phased me, then I was too hard. If I spoke about my past trauma, then I was too broken. Every inch of who I was became the reason why I was too difficult to love.

But I am slowly learning that you will never be too much or too little of anything, for the *right* person. When it's right, you will be perfectly enough for them. When it's right, you won't have to keep cutting away parts of your soul just to be loved and accepted. When it's right, they will embrace and complement your uniqueness. When it's right, you won't feel as though you are too much to deal with, or that you're asking for too much.

The right person will love you unconditionally, as the person you *truly* are.

Moving On Without an Apology

Sometimes we don't get an apology from the one who broke our heart, and so we must find a way to heal and move on without it. But from what I've learned of heartbreak, healing is not dependant on apologies, and they rarely occur simultaneously. So, you don't *need* an apology from them to let go of the hurt and move forward with your life.

When my first long-term boyfriend broke my heart after six years together, I somehow found the strength to let go of the pain and anger after a few short months, despite his lack of remorse for his toxic behaviour and infidelity. It wasn't until *years* later that he seemed to acknowledge the pain he'd caused me, and finally apologise. Although, when I did eventually receive that apology, it was very anti-climactic. I guess the fact that I had waited for it for so long had taken away its meaning and sincerity.

Then when my last relationship broke down because of his abusive behaviour, he apologised profusely, and repeatedly, for months directly after the breakup. Yet I could not find it in my heart to forgive him until almost a year had passed. I could not let go of the anger and resentment for so long, because the hurt was so much deeper than any heartbreak I'd ever experienced. And so, his apologies became nothing more than empty words, words that didn't ease even an ounce of the pain that crushed me.

In both of those breakups, their apologies and my healing were *not linear*. Because the truth is, an apology does not suddenly make everything okay, it won't instantly take away that pain from your heart. And so, we cannot delay our healing whilst we wait for an apology that may or may not come.

Retraining Your Brain After Abuse

I hope as you heal, you are able to *unlearn* everything that abusive relationships have taught you.

I hope you begin to understand that being treated with kindness and affection are a normal part of healthy relationships, not something you should desperately fight for or *earn*.

I hope you now recognise that extreme jealousy is incredibly toxic and destructive. So, if you find a lack of jealousy in a new relationship it does *not* mean that they don't care for you – or that the depth of their love is any weaker.

I hope you learn that living in a constant state of chaos is neither normal, nor healthy. I know the endless raging fights can seem like they stem from a place of deep passion, but please understand that you should not have to tiptoe around the one you love to keep their angry outbursts at bay.

I hope you learn to stop seeing the enemy everywhere you go. You are safe now – you don't have to avoid people out of fear, you don't need to flinch from someone's loving embrace. It was never fair for you to live in such fear, but know that you don't need to be so *afraid* anymore.

I hope you know that there are still good and kind people in this world who won't take pleasure in hurting you, who will do anything to see you smile, who will be gentle with your heart, and who will show you genuine love and respect without an ulterior motive.

These Feelings Can Co-Exist

You can love someone, but also hate the person they have become. You can fear walking away from a relationship, but also hope for the life you will build after them. You can miss someone, but still not want them to be a part of your life anymore. You can feel pain over the breakup, but also relief that it's over. You can grieve what the relationship once was, whilst still finding joy in your new reality.

Please don't convince yourself that you should feel a specific way once the relationship is over, or that certain feelings are more valid than others. I know it's confusing and frustrating to still love someone who broke your heart, yet also be incredibly angry at them. But please understand that conflicting emotions *can* co-exist. You're not supposed to instantly stop loving them the second you breakup, human emotions are complex, and you can't suddenly switch off feeling one thing in favour of another. The anger and sadness you now feel towards them does not cancel out the love you have felt for so long.

This understanding helped me so much during my last breakup. For weeks afterwards, I mentally punished myself for still loving the one who caused me nothing but pain. For still missing the one who brought so much chaos into my life. Until I began to learn that feelings are not simply *either/or*, they are *and*. I was heartbroken over walking away from him, *and* relieved that those years of pain were finally over. I felt fear about my future going forward *and* hope at what was still to come. I felt incredibly frustrated that I put my everything into a relationship that ultimately failed, *and* thankful for the lessons that experience ultimately gave me. I hated him for what he put me through, *and* I still loved him for all the beautiful moments we shared together.

You Don't Need Closure to Move on
And Heal

Sometimes the desire for closure after a breakup is so intense that it keeps you gripping on to the past, and prevents you from truly healing – the unanswered questions eating away at you, slowly destroying you from the inside. You loved them so much that you just can't comprehend why they gave up on you.

It's human nature to crave resolution to uncertainties, so you desperately search for answers as to *why* it had to end, and why you had to suffer like this. Or maybe you have some deep need to make them see how much they hurt you, and tell them everything you held back from saying during the relationship.

We live in a society where we have been led to believe that having all of the answers will bring you some sense of closure, that it will give you the peace you need to let go and move on. But let me be the first to say that the search for closure will not take away the hurt you feel after a breakup, and having answers to all of the *why's* will not soften the edges of your heartbreak.

The truth is, seeking closure from someone who broke your heart can be incredibly painful and cruel, doing more harm to you than good. And sometimes there are no answers – because things simply just happen, with no real explanation. Sometimes, there are no beautiful endings to a story. I know it's confusing, but please understand that no solid closure *is* the closure.

You may never know why they walked away, if they ever truly loved you, or why the relationship faded into nothing. But you don't *need* to know to close that chapter of your life and move on. So, please don't delay your healing by placing it in the hands of someone else, or making it dependent on answers you may never get.

I hope you know that only *you* can give yourself true closure, by choosing to let go of the past and focus on your healing. To accept that they were not your person, and that's okay, because there are still people in this world who will love you in the way that you deserve. Please, rather than letting the search for answers consume you, direct all of that energy inwards – to care for your heart in a way that they never did.

The Addictive Nature of Toxic Relationships

I hope you forgive yourself for staying in a toxic relationship longer than you should. I hope you learn to let go of the self-blame for not being able to break the attachment sooner, and before it consumed every inch of your heart and soul.

You see, toxic relationships are like addictions. Even if you come to realise, deep in your bones, that the one you love is bad for you; you somehow find yourself needing to hold on to them with every fibre of your being. That need overthrows all logic because the relationship has become your *drug*. A drug that you know is deeply harmful to you, but the highs keep you returning for more – as though you are trying to medicate the pain with the very person that keeps hurting you.

I know there is a part of you that keeps punishing yourself for staying with them, for choosing pain over healing. And so, you plead with your logic, desperately searching for answers of why you can't seem to walk away – *for good* this time.

I hope this knowledge eases some of the self-blame that consumes you: it's human nature to crave validation in relationships, it triggers a pleasure response in our brains. So, the more you experience chaos and unpredictability in a relationship, the more you *crave* the pleasure of their validation. When you crave something, your brain releases a shot of Dopamine – the happiness chemical – so that validation becomes your *high*, feeling like you need it as much as you need your next breath. And the unpredictability of not knowing whether they will show you affection or be completely cold also causes an Adrenaline release, which only intensifies the addiction to them even more.

The sad truth is, toxic people understand this pattern, and use it to their advantage. At the start of the relationship, they shower you with sweet words and endless affection, creating powerful feelings of desire in you. And then they stop. Suddenly and callously, leaving you reeling in the rejection. But the intense feeling of their 'love' still lingers in you, so you hold onto them, waiting for any scrap of attention they decide to give you. You suffer through the lows; anything to feel that *high* of their affection and validation again.

Not Everything We Love Is
Good for Us

Sometimes I still struggle with the idea that we are not always meant to love the ones we are drawn to, that they are not supposed to have a permanent place in our lives. Because I guess it makes no rational sense – how my soul could ache for someone who simply wasn't *good* for me.

And I think this is one of the reasons I held onto the relationship for so long, because how could I have such an incredibly deep connection with someone if it wasn't meant to last? Why did it feel like there was this undeniable magnetic force pulling us together, if it was healthier for us to be apart? How could I let go of someone who set my body and soul on fire, who made me feel *alive.*

But I am slowly learning that there is a vast difference between chemistry and compatibility. Chemistry is the force that pulls two people together, creating an explosive reaction. But compatibility determines if that intense pull will transcend into a healthy and long-lasting relationship – because sometimes, two elements just don't mix well together.

And the difficulty is, chemistry creates such powerful and passionate feelings within us, that it can cloud our judgement of whether the person we're drawn to will be a compatible part of our life in the long-term – if their values, lifestyle, or character actually align with our own. And so, we risk staying in a relationship that turns out to be unhealthy, destructive, or simply brings out the *worst* in us.

I eventually came to realise that I was not supposed to keep him in my life, that our entwined souls were never meant to linger, but the connection and pull that existed between the two of us made it almost impossible for me to let go – *for good*.

The Necessity of Forgiveness

I know it sometimes feels impossible to offer your forgiveness to the one who hurt you, especially when you're still haunted by the pain of their actions.

I know you might think that they don't *deserve* your forgiveness, when all you feel is anger towards them for how deeply they broke you, and all the promises they failed to keep.

I know forgiveness is that much harder when you never received an apology from them. So, you question how you can possibly offer forgiveness to someone who never showed a shred of remorse or regret – even as they watched you turn to ash as they burned you.

The truth is, forgiving someone doesn't mean that the pain they caused you was in any way acceptable, and it does not mean that you must immediately forget what happened. Rather, it's a means of letting go and cleansing your heart of the pain and anger you've held onto for so long.

So, forgiving the one who hurt you is more for your

own healing as it is for them. It might take time, and an immense amount of inner work. But it's necessary to truly forgive them so you can release the hurt and anger, slowly begin to heal your heart, and find the peace that you deserve.

Trying To Move On (When Their Hold Keeps Pulling You Back)

One of the hardest parts of moving on from a narcissist, is that they don't *want* you to move on – and so they do everything in their power to prevent you from moving forward in your life, and out of their grip of control.

Even if they were the one to end the relationship, you often find that they are incapable of letting you go completely. They continue to linger, trying to suck you back into a relationship, or to remain friends after the breakup – purely for selfish reasons.

And let me be the first to admit that this can make moving on feel almost impossible. When I ended my last relationship, my ex would find any reason or excuse to keep in contact with me, to remind me of his existence when I desperately wanted to forget. He tried to suck me back in with romantic gestures – long winding messages with promises to change, and sending me flowers on what would have been our anniversary. Showing up at places where he knew I would be, so that we would *unexpectedly* run into each other. Playing on my empathetic personality, by feigning situations or problems he needed my help with.

The fact is, narcissists are master manipulators, they know all of your deepest insecurities, and will use them to appeal to your emotions – to force their way back into your heart. Please, don't be fooled by their schemes to win access to you once more. Because as soon as they feel secure again, they will ultimately go back to that same cycle of tearing you down, and using you for their own benefit.

It took me longer than I care to admit, to realise that his persistent attempts to keep me in his life were not because he loved or missed me (like he *always* claimed), it was simply another power play. Because of their lack of empathy, relationships are simply transactional to narcissists, they see you as a supply for their ego rather than a human being. So they *need* to keep you in their life, to have your attention and validation, so they can avoid feeling their emptiness within.

When their attempts to suck you back into their life fail, their *true colours* begin to show. They often go out of their way to assassinate your character to others, or try to change the narrative of the breakup to make themselves seem like the victim – again, a tactic to try and prevent you from truly moving on. They are experts at using veiled threats, shame or guilt to wear down your resolve, anything to gain that grip of power and control over you again.

I know it can be incredibly hard to completely cut them out of your life, especially if you still love or have feelings for them, but I've learned that the only way to truly move on is by going no contact. That way, you sever their access to you, protecting your heart and mind from their manipulative attempts to pull you back in.

Loving The Right Person Will Feel Even More Profound

If you can love the wrong person so fiercely, then imagine how much love you are capable of feeling for the *right* person – and how deeply they will love you in return.

For so long you made someone who wasn't right for you the centre of your universe, giving them your entire self – heart, body and mind. So when it's over, it feels like you will never love anyone that intensely again. That you will never feel those butterflies in your stomach when you hear someone's name, or your heart skipping a beat when they look at you. You believe that the love you felt was as far reaching as love goes.

But it wasn't. How could it be, when you constantly questioned their feelings for you. How could it be, when you never felt worthy of being loved by them. How could it be, when you still laid awake at night agonising if love was supposed to hurt this much. How could it be, when they only ever loved you in half measures.

One day you will crash into someone who makes you forget everything you *thought* you knew about love. Someone who shows you how it feels to be loved unconditionally – and when this happens, you will love them even more profoundly than anyone before.

The Lasting Effects of Trauma on The Body

If you have experienced trauma in the past, from your body being hurt or taken advantage of in some way, then you probably understand how incredibly difficult it is to accept or maintain any type of physical intimacy in subsequent relationships.

For me, even a simple hug became uncomfortable. It felt like my body turned to stone at their touch, as though I subconsciously built an invisible barrier around myself whenever they got too close – a coping mechanism to protect myself, I soon realised. Pulling away and isolating myself was the only way I knew how to handle what had happened to me.

It's painfully hard because you desperately want to feel a deep connection with someone, but the thought of trusting them with your body just throws you into fight or flight mode. The reason for this is that a hormone released during physical intimacy – Noradrenaline – is the same hormone that floods your brain when you experience intense fear. And if you have experienced trauma in the past, then your brain can struggle to distinguish whether this hormone has been released due to fear or not.

For some people, the struggle may be with the idea of letting go – ultimately relinquishing control of your body. Because of your past trauma, your brain might consider this to be too dangerous. When this happens, it can make you feel physically or emotionally disconnected during intimate moments. And so sex starts to become a burden, a routine part of the relationship that you sometimes dread – yet you still *crave* that physical intimacy.

I know it's confusing, and I know it hurts; but I want you to understand that *it's okay* if you feel like this. Please don't feel guilty or judge your trauma response, you endured something that put your body through a huge amount of shock.

Please don't allow someone to pressure you into anything you are not fully comfortable with – move at your own pace, maintain open and honest communication, and don't be afraid to enforce your boundaries when needed.

Know that healing can be an incredibly tough and long process. There will be times when something triggers you, and there will be times when you experience flashbacks – but that doesn't mean that you aren't moving in the right direction. Please, just be patient with yourself through the healing. You *will* find peace in your own body again.

They Were Not Your One and Only Love

When you are struggling to move on from someone you thought was your soulmate, I want you to believe that you will have more than one *great love* in your life.

And that was one of the hardest parts of letting go after my last relationship. We had spent so many years together, and in that time, I honestly thought that he was the love of my life. And the *only* love of my life. The one I was meant to spend the rest of my days with. The greatest love I would ever experience.

But honestly, I loved someone deeply before him, and I know that I will love immensely one day after him.

The truth is, you will fall in love more than once in your lifetime. Each love will look and feel completely unique. Each love will teach you something different about yourself, about life, about relationships. Each love will shape you into the person you are supposed to become.

If you're struggling to move on from someone you

thought was your soulmate, I want you to know that it's okay to hold a small piece of them in your heart after they have gone. They were one of the great loves of your life, and parts of you were forever changed by loving them.

It's Brave to Keep Your Heart Open

You once opened your heart so freely, to experience the full force of love without hesitation. Only to then have your heart crushed by someone you thought would hold it with such care. I know how deeply it hurt you – the disrespect, the frustration, the broken promises, the *betrayal*. But please resist the urge to build walls around your heart, a fortress nobody could ever break through again.

I know you are afraid, and I know you only want to protect yourself from any future trauma. But by keeping your heart completely closed, you prevent yourself from ever having genuine connections, or experiencing the honest and *gentle* love that is still out there waiting for you. How sad it would be to never place your trust in anyone, to always assume that they are the villain in your story. To let the fear of heartache overwhelm you. To feel that sense of dread and unease in the pit of your stomach when anyone starts to get too close to you.

Please understand that you can't experience love

without also experiencing fear. The key is to let yourself feel the fear, and *embrace* it, not hide yourself away from it. To make the conscious decision to keep your heart open – despite the risk, despite the worry, despite the grief and anger it once felt. I hope you know that that it's incredibly brave to be open to love after experiencing such heartbreak. It's brave to make yourself vulnerable. It's brave to let someone in, to permit them to see *all* the parts of you. And it's brave to allow someone to hold the entirety of your heart again.

Love Is Not Supposed
to Be 'Crazy'

I am slowly learning that love is not supposed to be a raging storm. It should not be so consuming that you feel as though you're drowning, *suffocating*. It should not be a constant source of conflict, with sporadic highs. It should not trigger the worst in you, making you despise who you are when you're with them. It should not force you to hold your breath, for fear of the unpredictable and erratic emotions. It should not hurt more than it feels good.

I am slowly learning that we need to stop romanticising the idea of being *crazy in love*, and instead be open to love that is peaceful – that calms the storm inside of you, not provoke it.

Because when it's right, the love will feel like home – a *safe* place, not an emotional war zone. When it's right, love will be supportive and healing, and wholly good for your mental health. When it's right, love will be there to quietly hold you in your darkest moments. When it's right, love will allow you to breathe, it will feel like a deep inhale. When it's right, love will be accepting and forgiving. When it's right, love will be a steady flow, not a chaotic wave.

Holding On To The Pain

It was an awfully hard realisation to face, that I was delaying my healing after my last breakup.

In my conscious mind I thought that I was moving forward. I wanted to believe that the heartbreak was fading with each passing day, along with the memory of *him*.

But I eventually came to realise that I was not healing at all, I was subconsciously holding onto the pain, keeping the wounds open, because it was the only thing I had left of him – of *us*, of everything I hoped we would be but now never would. It didn't matter that I was the one who left, it did not make it any easier to let go; because my decision to walk away was made out of necessity, not out of want.

As the memories faded of what it felt like to be loved by him, to be in his embrace, to hear his booming laugh, to feel his hands running through my hair – the pain of what happened to us was my only reminder.

I desperately wanted to heal, but I just couldn't let go

of the hurt. Some part of me, deep down, didn't *want* to let go of that final piece that kept me tied to him, because then I would have to accept that it was truly over. I'd have to banish that small piece of hope in me that one day we would find our way back to each other.

But I am slowly learning that you can't make space in your heart or your mind for the love you deserve, if someone else is still being held there.

Time Is Not the Healer

I think many of us deeply believe in the myth that time is the greatest healer. That *just* time, and time alone, has the power to heal all emotional pain and trauma. That if we leave a wound alone for long enough, then eventually it will heal itself – the pain and suffering fading along with it.

But the danger of this belief is that it can prevent us from actively doing something to heal our trauma. So, we end up carrying the pain with us, sometimes for *years* to come. And no matter how much time passes, the wound remains open and aching – feeling like it happened only yesterday.

Maybe the passage of time will slightly take the edge off the pain, but the truth is – time itself is just a concept, it does not possess any healing power. It will not magically make everything okay. It's what we do with and within the time that truly matters. So, the nature of time is not to heal your emotional wounds *for you*, it's to give you the space you need to actively heal those wounds yourself.

In time – and *through* doing the hard inner work – we must build the strength to not simply endure the pain, but to release it from our hearts. In time, we must become more mindful of our emotions, rather than letting the days pass in a state of numbness. In time, we must learn to break the cycle of negative thought patterns. In time, we must find acceptance of everything that happened in the past, so it doesn't have the power to impact our future. In time, we must reach a state of forgiveness for those who made us suffer, letting go of the hate that consumes us. In time, we must discover who we are *after* the trauma, and how we want to live moving forward.

The point is, the simple passage of time is not enough, because emotional healing is a conscious process. So, in time we can heal our wounds – *if* we make the conscious decision to work on our healing within that time, to commit our energy and effort to it. This right here is the true healer.

Love, As A Whole

You can't choose certain parts of someone to love.

And I think that is one of the biggest mistakes we make in this generation of dating and relationships. We often fail to make the distinction between being *in* love and loving someone as a person and partner, which is necessary for lasting long-term relationships.

Falling in love is often emotionally intense, filled with excitement, passion and euphoria. Although, these types of feelings are often brief. But to truly love someone as a person, is to see and accept every fragment of who they are. The good *and* the bad.

If you honestly desire to spend your life with someone, you can't choose certain parts of them to love, whilst hating the others. Rather, you must look deeply into their soul, to see them as a whole and accept everything you find there. The light *and* the dark.

Why Empaths Need Boundaries

Your kind and compassionate heart is a true wonder in this harsh world. You choose to see the good in everyone, even in their darkest times, and that is a beautiful thing. But I hope you know that you can't have empathy without also having *boundaries*.

When you are an empathetic person, it can often feel incredibly difficult to set boundaries with the people you love. But please understand that boundaries do not mean that you have no empathy or compassion for others, they are simply there to protect your peace and your heart, to limit the impact you allow other people to have on you. You can still be there for them and offer your support, without sacrificing your own emotional wellbeing.

Boundaries are even more crucial if you find yourself in a toxic relationship. Because, as an empath, you will always find ways to justify their poor treatment of you. Without boundaries, your compassionate heart will be in danger of being used, abused and harmed – for their own selfish benefit.

That is why empaths and narcissists are often attracted to each other, but it's a dangerous combination. Your empathetic heart is *drawn* to their insecurities. You end up pouring your entire soul and energy into the relationship, because you truly believe that you can make them feel better about themselves. To change or heal them. But narcissists see empathy as a weakness and will use it to obtain every shred of love and attention they can get from you. Without boundaries, they will *consume* everything from you, until you are a shell of the person you once were.

A Heart Like Yours Deserves
a Love Like This –

A love that simultaneously makes you feel free *and* at home. A love that fills your heart as easy as the air fills your lungs. A love that excites you whilst also keeping you grounded. A love that makes you believe in love again. A love that fills your entire being, reaching the deepest corners of your heart and soul. A love that is truly unconditional. A love that never makes you feel like you're asking for too much, by simply wanting your needs met. A love that is there for you – any time, any place. A love that gives you the encouragement and space to grow into the best version of yourself. A love that makes your heart skip a beat when they look at you. A love that feels like both fire *and* water. A love that makes you feel wholly worthy of love. A love that breaks through all of the walls you built around your heart. A love that makes you deeply inhale and exhale when they hug you, as though you can finally breathe again. A love that looks deeply into your soul and accepts everything they find there. *A love that transcends space and time.*

Nostalgia Is a Seductive Liar

It's curious how nostalgia can be so pleasantly sweet at times, yet after a breakup it's often incredibly torturous. But I guess it makes sense, given that the Greek definition of nostalgia translates to *"the pain and suffering caused by yearning to return to the past"*. And oh, how I suffered in the aftermath of the breakdown of my last long-term relationship.

It seemed that wherever I went, and whatever I did, I was still haunted by the memory of *him*. I tried to erase all traces of the relationship from my life, but six months later I was still plagued by the memories deeply embedded in my mind. The deep sound of his voice when he called my name. The butterflies in my stomach when he absentmindedly winked when we locked eyes across a room. How it felt when his warm lips gently pressed against my forehead.

There seemed to be no remnants of his dark side in my memories, however. The pain and suffering I experienced in the relationship were conveniently forgotten, dead and buried somewhere in my subconscious. I forgot the constant fights. I forgot the

121

chaos and stress that came with the relationship. I forgot the nights I would lay awake praying for things to get better. I forgot what it felt like to cry myself to sleep. And that's the danger of nostalgia. It's a beautiful, seductive liar.

After a breakup, no matter how much your heart was torn to shreds in the process, your mind is often flooded by the reminder of everything you loved about them. You desperately try to move on, but the memories of those good moments together linger in your mind, forcing you to question whether the breakup was truly the right thing.

Ultimately, that is what makes nostalgia such a seductive liar – it distorts your memories. Missing the one you loved leads to your brain becoming *selective*. It replays the few good moments on a loop, whilst simultaneously removing the bad memories from your consciousness. Those few picture-perfect memories cause you to idealise them, painting the relationship in a way that is different to the reality. And so, we crave something that our mind tells us was beautiful. We crave the lie, a *delusion* forced upon us by our own memories.

I hope it helps you to know that experiencing nostalgia after a breakup does *not* mean that it was the wrong choice to end the relationship. It's simply a normal process that your mind goes through, as your memory system tries to make sense of the memories of someone who is no longer an integral and defining part of your life. Those memories were once an important part of the relationship, strengthening your bond through a shared history together. So now, your mind needs time to figure out where those memories fit.

I know right now the nostalgia feels like such torment, your own personal hell. But, please understand that it *will* pass. It *will* get easier. And the memory of them *will* slowly fade – by challenging the good memories with the bad. If you are missing and longing for someone who broke your heart, remind yourself of how they *really* made you feel in the relationship. Reach deep into your mind, and find a vivid memory that reminds you why the relationship did not work out. The more you practice this, the less your brain will be able to retrieve those beautiful memories you're being haunted by.

The Beauty in Being Alone

If you are holding onto someone who is not right for you simply because you fear being alone, I want you to know that there is a vast difference between alone and *loneliness* – and one does not necessarily equate to the other.

I had to learn this the hard way. My first long-term relationship began when I was seventeen years old, and lasted for six years – but it should have *never* survived for as long as it did. I held on for a number of reasons, but the main one being my fear of being alone after spending so many years of my life with someone. But, I learned that sleeping beside someone every night who makes you feel desperately lonely, is so much worse than being alone.

Let me be the first to say that it can be incredibly hard to find comfort in your own presence, especially if you have grown accustomed to being in a relationship with someone. I chose to move out of my parents' house at eighteen to live with him, to then find myself single at twenty-three and having absolutely no idea of *how* to be alone. Even though independence has been a key part of my personality since childhood, it still felt overwhelmingly uncomfortable and isolating to be alone for the first time. It was a scary and messy experience, but, it turned out to be one of the most valuable lessons in my life so far – because there is immense growth and *peace* to be found in solitude.

Being alone gives you the space to think, and to listen to your own thoughts without any outside influence. Here, you get to truly discover *who* you are when nobody else is around – your likes and dislikes, your wants and needs, your goals and dreams. Or, simply to find yourself again, if your identity was consumed by your last relationship.

Being alone gives you a sense of complete *freedom*. You are free to discover, create, travel, explore and learn – without anyone to answer to but yourself. Walking this path alone, even just for a while, is an incredible opportunity for self-discovery. For finding out where you truly belong in this world.

Being alone encourages you to properly heal your heart and mind after your last heartbreak, taking all of the love you gave to someone else and directing it back into yourself. Here, you are also able to discover healthy healing methods, rather than using a new relationship to distract you from the hurt.

Spending some time alone after a breakup also gives you the space you need to find clarity on the relationship, and to understand what your wants and needs are in a future partner – so you don't keep allowing people into your life who are not good for you.

Once you have found peace in the solitude, you will find yourself becoming much more selective about what and *who* you surround yourself with. Your inner harmony becomes so sacred, that you only choose to give your time and energy to people who are good for your mental health.

Remaining Soft When the World Tries to Make You Hard

The kindest hearts often have the deepest scars. The strongest hearts have sometimes experienced the most profound pain. The most beautiful souls are often those who have walked through the deepest pits of despair – and survived.

I know you did not choose to be where you are right now, suffering through this hurt. But please know that you do get to decide how you *respond* to the pain, and there is immense power in that. You can choose to let it make your heart softer, not hard. You can choose to become kinder and more compassionate, rather than hiding your beautiful heart behind an ice-cold wall. You can choose to let it fuel your growth, not tear you apart. You can choose to find strength through healing, rather than remaining broken by holding onto the hurt. You can choose to understand the purpose of the pain, and let it be your greatest teacher. You can choose to hold onto that spark of optimism, even when everything feels unimaginably hopeless.

I know it's hard to find the light when the pain feels so overwhelming, like a darkness spreading through everything good within you. But please understand that you now get to decide how this experience *shapes* you – and I hope you choose to remain soft in a world that constantly tries to harden you.

*

FRANKIE RILEY is a British writer and psychologist, and author of 'All The Dark Places' – a collection of poetry.

instagram.com/itsfrankieriley
tiktok.com/@wordsbyfrankie
medium.com/@frankie-riley

Printed in Great Britain
by Amazon

35913413R00078